A green car.

Cars

Written by Monica Hughes

Collins

A yellow car.

2

5

A black car.

7

A blue car.

9

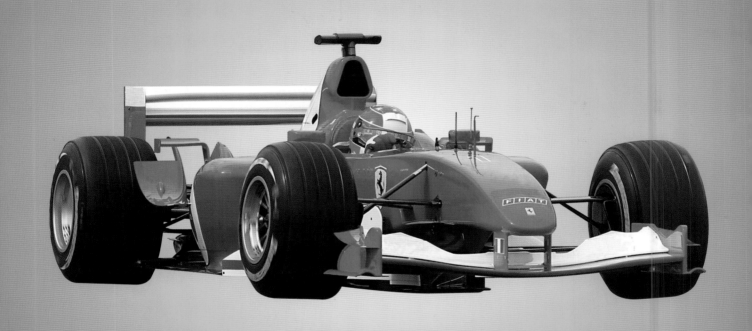

A red car.

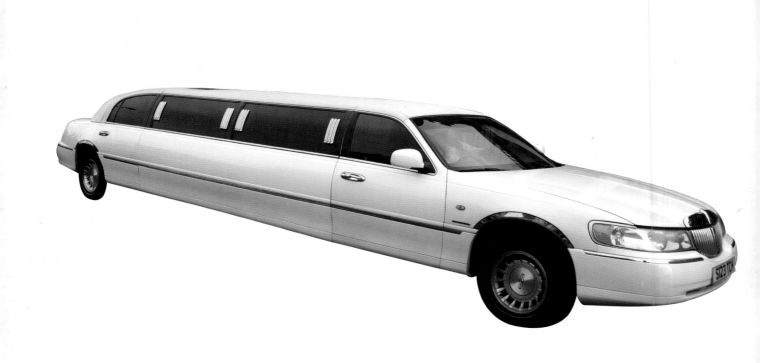

A white car.

13

Cars

yellow

green

black

blue

red

white

Ideas for reading

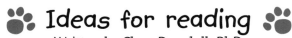

Written by Clare Dowdall, PhD
Lecturer and Primary Literacy Consultant

Learning objectives: Recognise printed words in a variety of settings, e.g. labels, captions; make collections of words linked to particular topics; extend vocabulary exploring the meanings and sounds of new words; use talk to organise, sequence and clarify thinking, ideas, feelings and events.

Curriculum links: Knowledge and understanding of the world: Look closely at similarities, differences, patterns and change

High frequency words: a

Interest words: car, yellow, green, black, blue, red, white

Getting started

- Look at the front and back covers of the book and talk about the car shown. Ask the children what they know about cars (e.g. they have wheels)

- Explain that you are going to find out about different cars by reading the book together. Read the blurb together. Make a list with the children of different cars.

- Read pp2–3 together, and model using your finger to match spoken to printed words. Model using the initial letters and the picture to read the word 'yellow'.

- Discuss the 'yellow' car, e.g. it is a taxi; it is in a city. What more can the children say about the car from the picture?

Reading and response

- Ask children to read the book independently and aloud. As they read, remind them to look at the pictures and the initial sounds to help them read the colour words. Praise children for one-to-one matching and using their finger.

- Ask them to use the right-hand pictures to find out information about the different cars (e.g. what they are used for, who drives them, how fast they go, how big they are).